DINOSAURS

LETTER TO PARENTS

Dear Parents,

Dinosaurs is an engaging early reader for your child. It combines simple words and sentences with stunning, life-like images of dinosaurs. Here are some of the many ways you can help your child learn to read fluently.

Before Reading
- Look at the book's cover together. Discuss the title and the blurb on the back.
- Ask your child what he or she expects to find inside.
- Discuss what your child already knows about dinosaurs.

During Reading
Encourage your child to:
- Look at and explore the pictures.
- Sound out the letters in unknown words.
- Use the glossary to learn new words.

Ask questions to help your child engage more deeply with the text. While it's important not to ask too many questions, you can include a few simple ones, such as:
- Where are the *Allosaurus's* claws?
- Would you like to have met this dinosaur? Why?
- Can you count the *Triceratops'* horns?

After Reading

- It is important to ensure that your child understands whole sentences and pages as well as individual words. As a comprehension check, ask a few questions about the content and encourage your child to tell you about the book.
- Provide opportunities for your child to read and reread the book. Praise your child's effort and improvement.

Sight Words

This page provides practice with commonly used words that children need to learn to recognize by sight. Not all of them can be sounded out. Familiarity with these words will increase your child's fluency.

Picture Dictionary

This activity focuses on learning vocabulary relating to dinosaurs. All the dinosaur names are featured in the book.

Glossary and Index

Encourage your child to use the glossary and index. Explain their purposes and that the entries are in alphabetical order. When your child is reading the book, point out that the words in bold type are the ones that are defined in the glossary.

DINOSAURS

Dinosaurs lived more than 66 million years ago. They were **reptiles**, like snakes and lizards.

Tyrannosaurus rex

Parasaurolophus

Brachiosaurus

Deinonychus

Allosaurus

TYRANNOSAURUS

(tye-RAN-oh-SORE-us rex)

T. rex was a meat-eater. It hunted other animals. This means it was a **predator**.

tooth

HOW BIG?

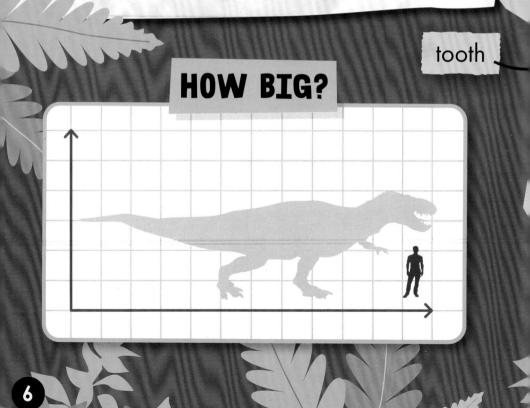

REX

eye

mouth

FUN FACT

Each *T. rex* tooth
was the size
of a banana.

STEGOSAURUS

(STEG-oh-SORE-us)

Stegosaurus ate plants. Animals that eat plants are called **herbivores**.

head

HOW BIG?

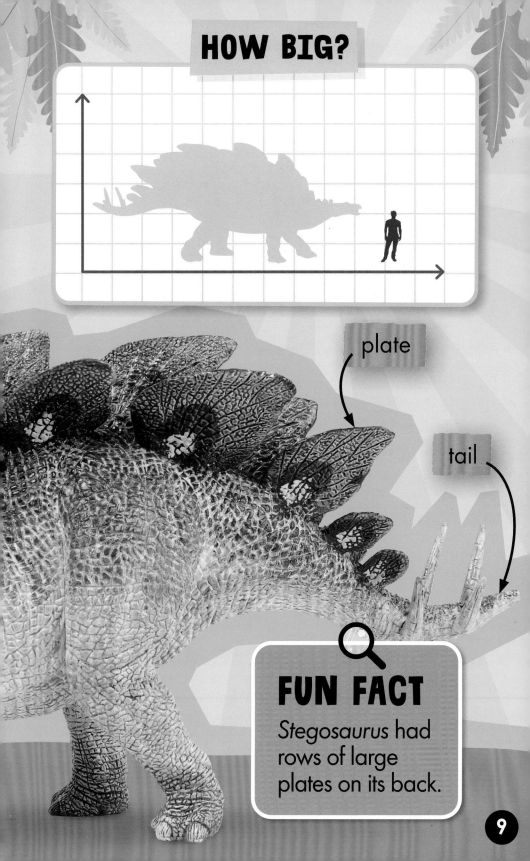

plate

tail

FUN FACT

Stegosaurus had rows of large plates on its back.

TRICERATOPS

(tri-SERR-ah-tops)

Triceratops had three horns on its head. Some horns grew as long as a baseball bat.

beak

HOW BIG?

frill

horn

FUN FACT

A *Triceratops* was as heavy as a pickup truck.

VELOCIRAPTOR

(vel-OSS-ee-rap-tor)

Velociraptor was a fierce dinosaur. It used its long back legs to chase **prey**.

FUN FACT

A *Velociraptor* was the same size as a turkey.

HOW BIG?

tail

back leg

feather

claw

BRACHIOSAURUS

(BRACK-ee-oh-SORE-us)

Brachiosaurus ate leaves at the tops of tall trees. It had a long neck and long front legs.

tail

neck

front leg

HOW BIG?

SPINOSAURUS

(SPINE-oh-SORE-us)

Spinosaurus ate meat. Meat-eating animals are called **carnivores**.

claw

HOW BIG?

sail

spine

FUN FACT

It had a tall, bony **sail** on its back.

ANKYLOSAURUS

(AN-kee-lo-SORE-us)

Ankylosaurus was covered in **armored plates**. The plates helped protect its body.

armored plates

horns

HOW BIG?

club tail

FUN FACT

Ankylosaurus was as big as a tank.

DEINONYCHUS

(die-NON-i-kus)

Deinonychus was fast and smart. Its body had feathers, like a bird.

tail

HOW BIG?

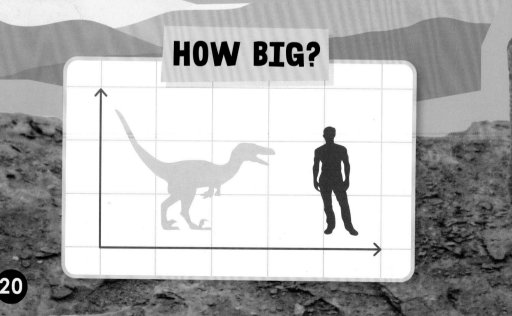

feathers

teeth

FUN FACT

Deinonychus means "terrible claw." This dinosaur had huge claws.

claw

PARASAUROLOPHUS

(pa-ra-SORE-OH-lo-fus)

Parasaurolophus had a long bone on top of its head. This bone is called a **crest**.

HOW BIG?

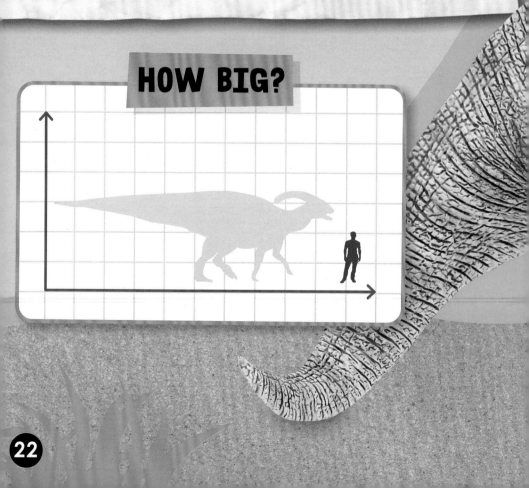

crest

beak

ALLOSAURUS

(AL-oh-SORE-us)

Allosaurus had sharp teeth that curved backward. It had three claws on each hand.

FUN FACT

Allosaurus hunted smaller dinosaurs.

claw

spines

hand

HOW BIG?

MORE PREHISTORIC CREATURES

All dinosaurs lived on land. **Reptiles** that flew or swam were not dinosaurs.

Elasmosaurus was a swimming **reptile**. It had a very long neck.

The pterodactyl was a flying **reptile**. It had a light body and big wings.

FUN FACT

Scientists think some birds are related to **prehistoric reptiles**.

SIGHT WORDS

Sight words are words that appear in most text. Practice them by reading these sentences. Then make more sentences using the sight words from the border.

Dinosaurs **lived** a long time ago.

Stegosaurus **had** large plates.

Ankylosaurus **was as** big **as a** tank.

THINK ABOUT IT

How much do you know about dinosaurs and prehistoric creatures? Try answering these questions. If you don't know an answer, look back in the book to find out more.

1 What did *Stegosaurus* eat?

2 Why might *T. rex* have scared other dinosaurs?

3 Would you like to fly like a pterodactyl? Why?

PICTURE DICTIONARY

Write the correct word under each picture to create your own picture dictionary.

egg   *Allosaurus*   tooth   horn   tail

tree   claw   wing   *Triceratops*

....

....

....

GLOSSARY

armored plate a patch or layer of thick bone that protects an animal

carnivore a meat-eating animal

crest a long bone or tuft of feathers on top of an animal's head

dinosaur an animal belonging to a group of reptiles that lived millions of years ago

herbivore a plant-eating animal

predator an animal that hunts and eats other animals

prehistoric from the time before people kept written records

prey an animal this is hunted and eaten by other animals

reptile a group of animals with scaly skin that lay eggs

sail a tall, thin layer of bone and skin sticking up from an animal's back

INDEX